Milly, Molly and Pennyr

"We may look different
but we feel the same."

In the early morning the cows came in to be milked. Milly and Molly liked to pull on their boots and hats to help.

Farmer Hegarty knew his cows by name and so did Milly and Molly. There was Buttercup, Blossom, Clover, Daisy and Pennyroyal.

"Come on, girls," Farmer Hegarty called. "Come on, girls," called Milly and Molly. The cows all smelled warm and grassy and blinked their eyelashes gently.

Well, not quite all... Pennyroyal was different.
She was always angry.
She wouldn't walk at the back.

She wouldn't walk in the front.

She refused to walk in the middle.

And she refused to stand still to be milked.

Pennyroyal grew more and more angry.
One morning she was so angry she lashed out
at the bucket.

"Pennyroyal," said Farmer Hegarty firmly.
"You're banished until you learn to control
your anger."

Pennyroyal was put out on her own.
"You can come back," Milly and Molly said
kindly, "when you smell warm and grassy and
blink your eyelashes gently."

Pennyroyal turned purple with rage.
She tore at the grass.

She charged at the fence.

And she chased Farmer Hegarty all the way
home.

Farmer Hegarty came out with his mirror.
"There you are, Pennyroyal," he said.

Pennyroyal looked at her angry face and hung her head low with shame.

From that day on, she walked at the back.

She walked in the front.

She was happy to walk in the middle.

And she stood as still as she could to be milked.

Farmer Hegarty patted her gently when she didn't lash out at the bucket. "Well done, Pennyroyal, you've learned to control your anger."

"You smell warm and grassy," whispered
Milly and Molly. And Pennyroyal blinked her
eyelashes gently.

Farmer Hegarty knew all his cows by name
and so did Milly and Molly.
There was Buttercup, Blossom, Clover, Daisy
and Pennyroyal.

"Come on, girls," Farmer Hegarty called.
"Come on, girls," called Milly and Molly.
The cows all smelled warm and grassy and
blinked their eyelashes gently.